To: Jay—

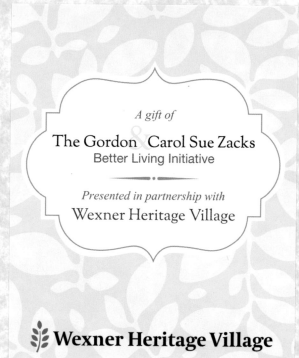

A gift of

The Gordon & Carol Sue Zacks
Better Living Initiative

Presented in partnership with
Wexner Heritage Village

🌾 **Wexner Heritage Village**

L'Chaim,
Cathy Zacks
Gildenhorn

Redefining Moments
End of Life Stories for Better Living

GORDON B. ZACKS

EDITED BY CATHERINE ZACKS GILDENHORN

Author's profits from the sale of this book are being donated to charity.

Library of Congress Cataloging-in-Publication Data is available.
ISBN: 978-0-8253-0735-5

Other Books by Author:
Defining Moments (2006)

For inquiries about volume orders, please contact:
Beaufort Books
27 West 20th Street, Suite 1102
New York, NY 10011
sales@beaufortbooks.com

Published in the United States by Beaufort Books
www.beaufortbooks.com

Distributed by Midpoint Trade Books
www.midpointtrade.com

Printed in Canada

Content Design by Michelle Rousseau Laytner, Art Catalyst
Art Direction and Design by Rebecca Luttrell
Additional Design by Caroline Bounds and Allysa Wolf

Photo credits: Leslie Lane Photography, Getty Images, AP Images, and
Shutterstock (individual photo credits listed in back of book)

INTRODUCTION

Joseph Lieberman

U.S. Senator (Retired), Fellow – American Enterprise Institute,
Vice-Presidential Candidate (2000), and
Senior Counsel, Kasowitz, Benson, Torres & Friedman.

In *Redefining Moments*, we are invited to share in the final days of a great man, Gordy Zacks, and to appreciate his insights, his challenges and—most of all—his joy, his exhilaration, and his gratitude for a life well lived.

Gordy helped many people from many walks of life to better define their lives – their sense of purpose and their pursuit of happiness. He forever encouraged people to ask penetrating questions. In life's final moments, when others might avoid tough-minded inquiry, Gordy was fearlessly direct in getting others to deal with topics like the perceived humiliation of increased dependency on others. He grappled with big-picture questions about closure and purpose. In Gordy's world, people don't just have the right to human fulfillment in their lives. They, indeed, have the responsibility to focus on how their life can make a difference, often in tiny but meaningful ways.

Gordy Zacks loved and served America, Israel, and the Jewish people. By his own hard work and creativity, he achieved great success and then he shared that success with the larger community and world. I was proud to be Gordy's friend and honored to be asked to write this introduction. This man made an enormous difference for the better, and we are all the better because of him.

The end of life is usually a sad and somber time but in his final days and in this memorable book, Gordy Zacks lifted the shroud. He invites us to share moments of joy and to be inspired to give and take as much as we can from each moment of our lives. *Redefining Moments* is eloquent, direct, and moving. It is as unique and upbeat as Gordy, and as strong.

Thank you Gordy. God bless you.

Note: Dedicating this book and selecting the photo that would be used to accompany it were among the last decisions Gordon Zacks made in the final days before he left us on February 1, 2014.

This book is dedicated to my family.

Providing the opportunity and structure for the future may be the official purpose of family. This hardly does justice to the caring, the inspiration, and the love that keep families going. They give the greatest energy to life itself – perhaps no more so than in life's final stages. Our family has been an incalculable blessing at the end of life, first for Carol Sue and now for me. L'Chaim to life!

Top row: Cathy, Michael, Edward, and Elissa
Bottom Row: Carol Sue (of blessed memory), Kim, Ariela, and Gordy

Photo by Leslie Lane Photography

A Note to Readers

*This book intentionally
preserves a mixture of tenses.*

*The core of the book was written and
spoken by Gordy while he was alive. Parts
of it were finalized after his passing.
In some cases, the present tense remains
appropriate for dialogues and comments
that occurred while Gordy was with us.*

*Many comments contributed by
others in this book were drawn from
Celebration of Life events which gathered
together family, friends and associates
during Gordy's final days.*

End of life:

Death will be no stranger for any of us.

Coming to terms with the end of life
early and constructively can release
considerable positive energy.

It also helps many people grapple with
significant life planning. Having a positive,
clear-headed view of death may help others to
live a better, more fulfilling life themselves.

It's in that spirit that the observations, questions,
and experiences of the following pages are offered.

Taking Root:
Ideas of Goodness, Acts of Kindness

- Gordy

1

PURPOSEFUL LIVING:

WHEN THE MIRROR ON THE WALL TELLS YOU A NEW STORY

*Especially when facing dramatic
and unexpected situations,
Gordy's reliable response was to
remain calm and to assess the situation
for the positive opportunities that it
presented. So it was when Gordy
learned from his doctors that he
had mere weeks to live.*

*Gordy prioritized and determined
how he could best use the
remaining time in a purposeful way.
His decision: He would write a book
about end of life as he was about to
experience it. Gordy's hope was to spur
discussion about end-of-life opportunities.
He wanted his book to be the beginning of
a new conversation. It set the stage for the
creation of www.redefiningmoments.org,
a website where ongoing dialogue
is encouraged and open to people
of all faiths and backgrounds.*

You can't play games with yourself when the clock is ticking its last, but that doesn't have to translate to submission, defeat, and dread. It's been a wonderful life, and I'm thankful for every minute of it.

It's been a
wonderful life.

I'm thankful for
every minute of it.

Embrace Your Passions Through Your Values

As I approach the end of life now, it seems as inevitable as it is continuous with life itself...as necessary to renewal as any facet of the structure of life itself...as vital as every other part of the process of living itself. **If you have lived your life with passion and joy...and are approaching the end of life, stay true to your passions.**

Embrace your passions on every level and in every direction—your family every bit as much as your profession...your friends as much as your community...the person you are down deep as much as the roles you feel obliged to play. If I have learned one thing in these revealing days, it's: *Don't stop now!*

If I have learned one thing in these revealing days, it's:

Don't stop now!

Unexpected Death - A Reflection

How we view mortality is usually deeply informed by our earliest direct experiences with death. Assumptions—both negative and perhaps positive—are created that may be submerged in our awareness. My first real, personal encounter with death occurred at 5 AM on the morning of September 29, 1965. It was then I learned my father, Aaron Zacks (of blessed memory), had passed during the previous night.

We had just celebrated my father's 58th birthday the day before. My brother Barry was 29, and I was 32 years old. My father went to bed happy, healthy, and joyful. He never woke up, succumbing to heart failure. **He had no chance to say goodbye.**

Barry and I came together at Mom and Dad's home. He and I shared the same conclusion: **Before my Dad left us, there was nothing left unsaid**... nothing between Dad and God...nothing between Dad and us...nothing unsaid between Barry and me.

From our earliest years, our parents never let us go to bed angry with any other member of the family. We had to kiss and make up before we slept. We were never haunted by what was left unsaid. **What a great life lesson!**

Thank God Dad and Mom taught us this. Otherwise, you can't imagine how many psychologists we would have kept busy in our lifetimes...trying to expunge our guilt.

My father was a great man
of uncommon insight...

a man who endlessly gave
unconditional love.

During the day, every day,
tell your kids you love them.

Neither Barry nor I believed we would wake up on our 59th respective birthdays. He did not. On August 3rd, 1990 Barry (of blessed memory) died at the age of 54. **When I awoke on my 59th birthday, it was as if I had been reborn.**

My father was a great man of uncommon insight...a man who endlessly gave unconditional love – a very rare quality. My brother and I thought about him every day of our lives...and I still do today.

My father's death taught me two precious lessons. **First, we have no contract on how long...on how... on where or when life will end. Second, act as if today may be the last**...Don't just think that sentiment. Live it in every little gesture and expression. Have kids end the day with making up. And during the day, *every day*, tell your kids you love them.

11

Every Family Needs Closure

"My grandfather Gene and I had dinner at Legal Seafoods in Boston. It was the first and only time a one-on-one of this sort ever happened. The two of us just hung out together. Granddad gave me advice about myself, about life, about my sisters. We put away a couple of beers and downed a couple of lobsters.

"Granddad wasn't sick. There was no ominous foretelling of the future. This was just a grandfather and a grandson getting together, but Granddad died unexpectedly a week later. His death was on nobody's radar. Not mine. Not his. Nobody's.

"People often say of friends and relatives who have passed: 'I wish I had one more opportunity to see them, to ask them this, or to tell them that...' How fortunate I was to have that meal. For me, it has become an unforgettable moment in my life."

– Jack Ribakoff

Chances are your need for closure may be greater than you might recognize.

Chances are you'll remember this for the rest of your life and it may change your life.

Chances are you'll never have another chance.

"My first impression of Gordy Zacks? Preposterous."

- Les Wexner

Les Wexner is founder of the Limited Brands and the serial innovator who rejuvenated Abercrombie & Fitch and has dazzled us with creations like Victoria's Secret.

"My first impression of Gordy Zacks? Preposterous. I had never been anywhere in the world. What did I know? He told me stories about Golda Meir…and the Syrian ambassador. He said I should meet Rabbis David Hartman and Herb Friedman. Why don't I go to South Africa and get to know lay-leader Mendel Kaplan? Gordy has always been wonderfully preposterous in the way he has stretched my world. A common thread characterized Gordy, Herb Friedman, and Max Fisher—consistent, genuine purpose and consistent, genuine love. That's a combination that changes lives. It changed mine. Otherwise, I'd still just be selling sweaters. Be on the lookout for that rare coupling of traits in people you meet: a preposterously expansive vision coupled with consistent and genuine purpose and love. It can change lives…as it changed mine."

- Les Wexner

*"Be on the lookout for that rare coupling of traits
in people you meet: a preposterously
expansive vision coupled with consistent and
genuine purpose and love.*

It can change lives ... as it changed mine."

          - Les

It isn't what you do.

It's how you might help others to do more or better, if only for the reason that they may be doing it and teaching what they've learned...long after you're gone.

When Les appeared at the Celebration event, he said to me, "**Gordy, you changed my life.**" I told him that was the *secondary* achievement. "Les," I said, "the great accomplishment was that *you* changed the world." In the end, what you yourself do matters little. If you can help others just a little bit to do something bigger than life, then you have discovered and applied the principle of human leverage. Another end-of-life realization: It isn't what *you* do. It's how you might help others to do more or better, if only for the reason that they may be doing it and teaching what they've learned...long after you're gone.

"Leonard, have you met my Gordon yet?...

When you do, your life will never be the same."

- Florence Zacks Melton (of blessed memory)

"Back in the early sixties, Florence Zacks Melton, Gordy's mother, took my face in her hands and asked, 'Leonard, have you met my Gordon yet?' I wasn't sure, I told her. 'When you do,' she promised, 'your life will never be the same.'

"What a goal we all might aspire to:

To be for others that positive little difference that touches their lives and makes them not quite what they were the moment before."

- Leonard Bell

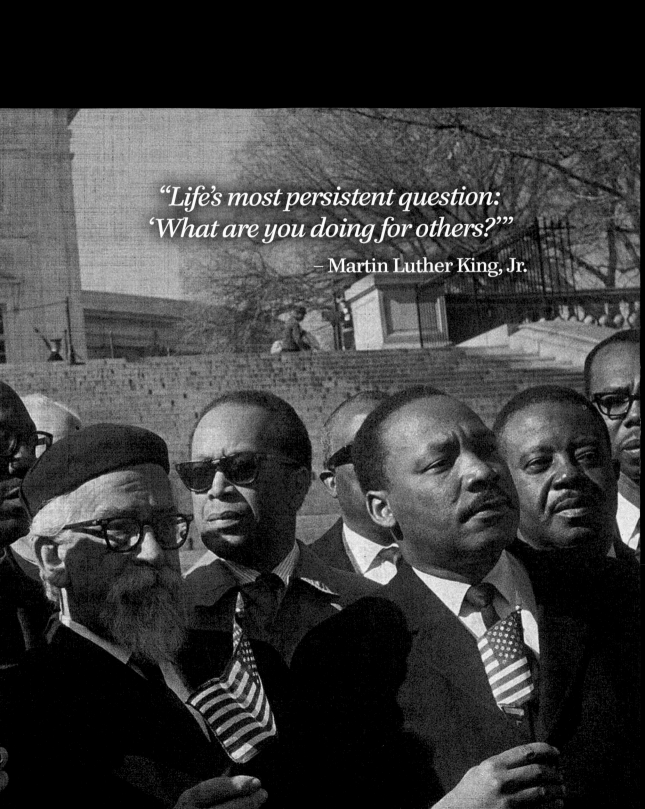

"*Life's most persistent question:
'What are you doing for others?'*"

– Martin Luther King, Jr.

"This one guy jumps into the water. You know who he is. The waters part and the people of Israel go forward on dry land. Given the time and the chance, it might have been Gordon Zacks jumping in first, helping us to make the way.

"Maybe it could be any one of us – given the right moment and the right time. Through strength and self-confidence and the willingness to risk, it lies within each of us to touch others, to change others... and even to change the world."

- Rabbi Harold J. Berman

I discovered my own life purpose
at age 15 – the rebirth of the Land and
the redemption of the People of Israel.

I discovered my own life purpose at age 15—the rebirth of the Land and the redemption of the People of Israel. Surely awareness of the Holocaust was a major drive in my commitment. I am especially struck now at how central this theme is to remembrance of the Exodus passage each year at Passover.

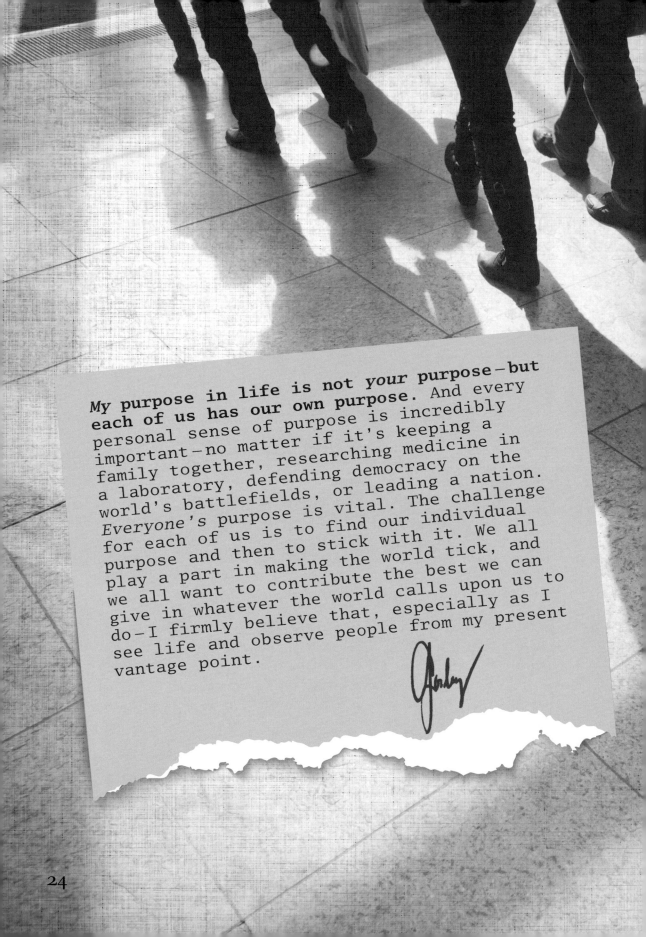

My purpose in life is not your purpose—but each of us has our own purpose. And every personal sense of purpose is incredibly important—no matter if it's keeping a family together, researching medicine in a laboratory, defending democracy on the world's battlefields, or leading a nation. Everyone's purpose is vital. The challenge for each of us is to find our individual purpose and then to stick with it. We all play a part in making the world tick, and we all want to contribute the best we can give in whatever the world calls upon us to do—I firmly believe that, especially as I see life and observe people from my present vantage point.

We all play a part in making the world tick, and we all want to contribute the best we can give in whatever the world calls upon us to do.

A Cherished Friend

About three weeks before Gordy's passing, Natan Sharansky flew in from Israel to pay Gordy a visit. An Israeli hero and human-rights activist, Natan's cause and liberation changed the course of Soviet East-Bloc and world Jewry in the twentieth century. The two talked for hours and spent more time discussing the future than they did reminiscing about the past.

The Future,
Not The Past

Natan observed: "The Holocaust was an incredibly powerful event, but we **Jews must rely on other more positive foundations to define ourselves in the future."**

"And we have a real opportunity to do so," Gordy responded. **"Israel is perhaps the greatest single human rights achievement of the 20th century.** That landmark was reached when the UN enabled the creation of the State of Israel. But we Jews have an enormous educational challenge yet to master. We have not equipped our young people to express or defend this viewpoint. That's one motivation why young people find exotic, esoteric belief systems an appealing alternative."

....

In the last stages of life, the focus shifts to the bigger picture challenges and opportunities that make a difference.

....

"And it's also a reason why it's relatively easy to dedicate oneself to causes like environmentalism," noted Natan, "and to do so to the exclusion of other priorities. Everyone wants both freedom and purpose. Freedom usually wins out for younger people. Then you discover that you need the grounding of a goal, especially when you have children."

"When you're looking at issues like this in the rear view mirror as I am today, it's easy to have a clearer grasp of the profile that they take and perhaps of their significance as well," Gordy commented. **"No matter what the issue—family relationships or international affairs— in the last stages of life, the focus shifts to the bigger-picture challenges and opportunities that make a difference."**

When you're looking at issues like this in the rear view mirror as I am today, it's easy to have a clearer grasp of the profile that they take and perhaps of their significance as well.

The Power of Little Things

GORDY: Few people excite in me such admiration as Natan Sharansky. Three-million Soviet bloc Jews were liberated as a result of the courageous initiative Natan's case dramatized. In Jewish history, that event is every bit the scale of the estimated 3 million Jews rescued in the Exodus and the 6 million ruthlessly slaughtered in the Holocaust.

NATAN: Sometimes I make a wisecrack: 'Gordy Zacks helps to set up one little meeting, and we are slaves to him for the rest of our lives!' And, you know what? I love this man – this man of action, with his relentless grasp of the big picture.

"Sometimes I make a wisecrack: 'Gordy Zacks helps to set up one little meeting, and we are slaves to him for the rest of our lives!'"

- Natan

Would there be a Google today

if 6-year-old Sergey Brin—later Google's co-founder—had not been permitted to emigrate to the United States? (Even straight-A Jewish students were systematically deflected from graduate school under the Soviet regime.)

Would the very idea of a watershed breakthrough like Google even be fathomable in the crumbling, cold, gray world of the Soviet Union?

A few little things are all that almost all of us are ever able to do to help make the world a better place. But Natan, he changed the world!

GORDY: In helping to arrange a White House meeting during the Reagan era, I played a small role that advanced Natan's case and that of Soviet Jewry on the global agenda. A few little things are all that almost all of us are ever able to do to help make the world a better place. But Natan, he changed the world!

31

People – I'm talking people of all sorts and at every level of human activity – are doing millions of things to make the world a better place. **Were that not so, the world would be mired in apathy or worse.**

32

"The opposite of love is not hate,
it's indifference."
– Elie Wiesel

The Power of Failure

My dad came west in a sheep rail car after graduating high school. My mother, probably the best educated person and the most fervent advocate of continuing education I have ever known, had to drop out of high school before receiving her diploma. She had to help earn rent money for the family. As a kid, we moved around a lot. After my birth in Terre Haute, Indiana, the family spent time in both Hagerstown and Cumberland, Maryland, and Steubenville, Ohio. Then we settled in Columbus, Ohio, where I went to 5 different schools.

My brother Barry and I knew we were going to college, we just never knew which one. By high school, I was in Bexley High, a good school, but I had no framework for selecting a college. I applied where my friends did: Ohio State, Harvard, and Dartmouth. I was accepted at Ohio State and Dartmouth, but rejected at Harvard. Thinking I was a pretty good guy, I called up Harvard to find out why they didn't want me. At first, I got a second brush-off. The admissions director wouldn't tell me. *"How the hell will I ever get better if you won't let me in on how I come up short?"* In a phone call the following day, he revealed to me that my SAT English scores weren't up to Harvard's standards either for getting in or staying in *that* school.

How will I ever get
better if you won't let me in
on how I come up short?

(from a call made to Harvard's admission director)

From that experience, I learned
it was important to fail in order to win.

Thanking him, I then figured if my English wasn't good enough to get into Harvard, it wouldn't be good enough to stay in Dartmouth. My entire schooling had been public to that point. Sumner Dennett, the Headmaster at the private Columbus Academy tested me. The summer between my senior year at Bexley and my freshman year at Dartmouth, I got a concentrated tutorial in English from Professor George Bown, the leading secondary-school English teacher in central Ohio. I broadened my skills considerably. **Today I have been known to remind professional writers with whom I've worked about the finer points of grammar.**

From that experience, I learned it was important to fail in order to win. It certainly taught me the fundamentals of English. Even more, it taught me the power of failure to personal development. Today, I stress to young people: Accept failure as a part of winning.

The Talmud does not say we are
obliged to finish what we start. It does say
we are obliged to make a beginning.

The Talmud does not say we are obliged to
finish what we start. It *does* say we are
obliged to make a beginning. **Be honest
about what you believe you have achieved
in your life. Most importantly, if you
believe you could have done a better job
or done things in a different way, share
your insight with others.** You spent an
entire lifetime capturing this hard-
earned wisdom, and it can be enormously
valuable to others you know who are
trying to achieve similar goals.

Priority and Purpose

1. Do I feel my overarching purpose "in the moment" in my last days with the same intensity that I have pursued it throughout my life?

2. Without trying to overdo what's possible, am I completing the last tasks I feel I must complete to leave life fullfilling the obligations I have committed myself to shoulder?

3. Have I asked for help from others when I recognized that I can no longer personally achieve goals that I have always assumed were my personal obligation?

4. Have I honestly accepted the fact that I will leave things undone … Instead of ruing that reality, have I done my best to entrust tasks and responsibilities to others who can continue my dreams in life when I will no longer be able to?

5. If I have felt remorse or regret about not achieving certain things in my life, have I come to terms with accepting these disappointments? Am I now focused on the positive and doable, instead of dwelling on sadness over lost opportunities?

6. If end of life is not an imminent issue for me now, do I still give purpose the priority it deserves in my daily living?

Growth is our opportunity to grow into the future, growth of a people, growth of a nation, and seeding future generations.

- Gordy

A POWERFUL SYNERGY: LOVE AND PURPOSEFUL LIVING

As the days advanced, Gordy continued his life-long absorption with "big-picture" topics. As one example, he thought intensely about the right balance between love and purpose in life.

During moments when his energy was strong, he still enjoyed engaging others in animated discussions. Topics such as education and the needs of future generations were top-of-mind concerns for him.

While serious issues commanded his attention much of the time, so did human love and awareness. He would often interrupt a discussion about weighty ideas with a request for a hug and a kiss from his young granddaughter Ariela.

Love may be the bedrock of
a fulfilling life when it is the Yin.

Purposeful Living may be the bedrock
when it is the Yang.

Love and Purpose–
The Balance

In recent days, my lady friend Gale Shamansky and I had a serious and lively conversation in the shadows of death. Our goal: Could we mutually agree on a definition of a fulfilling life?

Gale believed the cornerstone of a fulfilling life must be Love. Love in all its forms: **loving**... **being** loved...**sharing** love...**spreading** love.

As you might imagine, I had a different view: The cornerstone of life is Purposeful Living–doing things that benefit others. Our purpose is to make the world a better place.

Suddenly...like a bolt out of the blue, the ancient Chinese symbols of Yin and Yang occured to both of us. This icon not only depicts the collision of opposites. It also describes how the two contrary forces merge into each other. This fused image portrays change as rapid and never ending. It also presents change as a spiral, not a predictable straight line.

A fulfilling life needs the anchor of love,
but that love must fuel purposeful living.

Love a–n–d Purposeful Living.

Suddenly something was clear to us:

- Love may be the bedrock of a fulfilling life when it is the Yin.

- Purposeful Living may be the bedrock when it is the Yang.

Here are two crucial end-of-life lessons: While their truth might be especially vivid as the end of life approaches, the ideas are well worth putting to work at any point you may be on in life's journey. A fulfilling life needs the anchor of love, but that love must fuel purposeful living. Love **a-n-d** purposeful living. The one energy and drive feeds the other if we are to make the world a better place for others as well. The sooner a person realizes and harnesses the dual forces of love and purpose, the likelier they are to live a meaningful and constantly energized life.

The Union of
Purpose and Love

At times like this and especially at Shabbat, there has always been the union of pleasure and dialogue, this perfect marriage of purpose and love in life.

Yin and Yang capture the dialogue of life.
The dynamic is as real and vital in how we
engage our children as it is in the love
with our spouses or companions. In my closing
days, my daughters Cathy and Kim and I
reminisced about our sessions after Hebrew
Sunday school. Eating Whoppers from Burger
King in an old meeting room in the basement
of our home, we examined the nature of man
and the quest for purpose. At times like this
and especially at Shabbat, there has
always been the union of pleasure
and dialogue, this perfect marriage
of purpose and love in life.

A Dad with Great Spirit

"For me, it was the most magical Shabbat ever."

- Kim

"**Life is all about love, purpose, gratefulness and family.** Let me share something about when I was about 19-years-old and confused. I was living in Jerusalem and developed an interest in Judaism, so much so that I became a student at a religious institute there. At one of the lectures, I was told if a non-Jew was drowning on Shabbat, you don't save him because a Jew should only save the life of another Jew on Shabbat. I was very upset, so I called my dad and shared my grief and dismay. I did not expect that the next day I would open the door and see him standing before me. He flew in from Columbus, Ohio to Jerusalem just to spend Shabbat with me!

"For me, that was the most magical Shabbat ever. Every time I walk into the Old City in Jerusalem, I relive that moment … and I think that he does too. This experience captures the dedication my dad has to his family. He is a dad with great spirit, and it's our challenge as we follow him to fill that spirit.

"Time for me no longer means past, present, and future. It's the depth of the moment and its meaning. When I think about death, as all of us in the family have done recently, what comes to my mind is what my dad taught me about life. 'Remember me in life,' he says. **Showing me how to live…that's the best gift a father can give any child.**"

- Kim Zacks

"*Showing me how to live…
that's the best gift a father can give any child.*"
— Kim

If you save one life,
then you save the whole world.

That Shabbat in Jerusalem was one of the most powerful days of my life. When my daughter called and told me what she had been told, Kimmy said, "If that's what Jews believe, then I'm not Jewish." I nodded and agreed, "If that's what Jews believe, then I'm not Jewish either." When I went to Jerusalem, I said we should find someone who could straighten us both out. We went to see Rabbi David Hartman, the rabbi and contemporary Jewish philosopher. He spent the whole Shabbat with us and acknowledged what Kimmy heard was indeed in the Talmud, but that the Talmud also says, "If you save one life, then you save the whole world." What color, denomination or religion makes no difference. Human life is a gift created by God. That's a Judaism I get...that I understand. Kim and I both stayed in the fold. The experience was a revelation of what it takes to be a parent and when it's necessary for parents to be an example and to take uncommon steps. **For me that experience was the most important single moment of parenting I ever did—and the result: the daughter I am so very proud of today.**

The greatest gift Carol Sue gave me was two outstanding daughters.

In nearly six decades of a wonderful marriage, the greatest gift Carol Sue gave me was two outstanding daughters. The second was the personal space that she lovingly gifted me, and I believe I granted her comparable space in return. We were able to recognize and satisfy each other's needs: my passion for Israel, organizing programs, and teaching...her inexhaustible appetite for travel and adventure. Whether it was boating alone down the Amazon or backpacking through the Scottish Highlands with Kimmy, I understood how vital this was to her sense of purpose, and I could trust her to master every challenge well. It's this perpetual readiness to compromise coupled with deep love and trust that permits relationships to stay vital and energizing.

Gordon

The second was the personal space that she lovingly gifted me, and I believe I granted her comparable space in return.

...two people give and nurture and share,
Building and growing from mistakes in the past,
Planning together for things that will last.

– from a poem by Florence Zacks Melton,
Gordy's mother

"Two people can constructively pursue
a sense of purpose without them
sharing exactly the same purpose."

- Natan

The Harmony of Love and Purpose

"Two people can constructively pursue a sense
of purpose without them sharing exactly the
same purpose. The purposes can be congruent,
but they need not necessarily be identical. My
wife Avital's sense of purpose is driven forcefully
by dedication to religion. Mine is shaped more
by a sense for history. But it's still possible to
harmonize the two different approaches and
help each other realize this all-important quest
for purpose."

- Natan Sharansky

QUESTIONS TO CONSIDER:
Balance

1. Do I weigh how I spend my time and my energy between love and purpose?

2. When I consider my sense of purpose today, am I bitter or unhappy about what I might not have attained or had the opportunity to do? Do I instead find energy and motivation in those things I can still achieve and contribute— no matter how small they may seem?

3. Do I remind myself how easy it is to give love lip service and squander valuable time on actions more related to how I will be remembered than in positively impacting the lives of people I will leave behind?

4. Am I starving others of the opportunities for the love they want and deserve to give me in the ways they know best and mean the most to them?

5. Trying to be brave and valiant, do I starve myself of the love and understanding I really need, dismissing that need as unimportant versus other priorities?

6. Do I respect that other people may be caught up in genuine feelings of sadness? Do I do my best to help them see beyond the sadness and to focus on realizing the opportunities of the future?

*The process of growth is itself
a series of redefining moments.*

- Gordy

CELEBRATING LIFE:
REDEFINING
HOW WE LOOK AT
END OF LIFE

As part of his final days,
Gordon invited family, friends, and
associates he had known over decades to
his home. They shared stories, love, lessons,
and laughter in a series of memorable
Celebration of Life events.

Most of the comments contributed by others
in this book were drawn from spontaneous
remarks made at these gatherings.

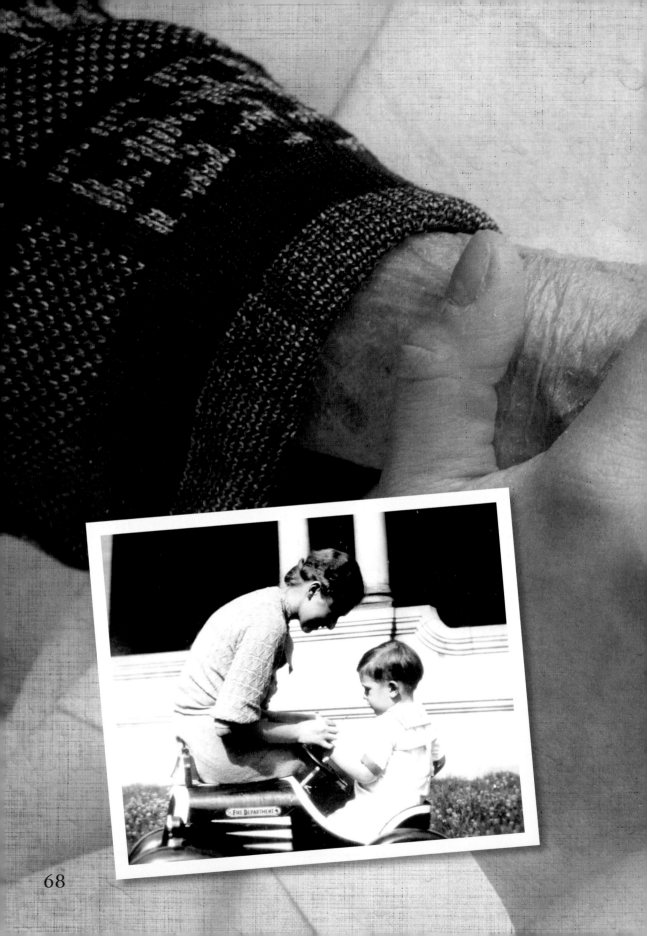

If I have touched your life, my friends,
Remember that you've touched mine.
And, if together we've changed the world a bit,
We've all been touched by the Divine.

– from a poem by Florence Zacks Melton,
Gordy's mother

When you talk with someone in the final stages of life, in a way you are talking with someone on the doorstep of being called back to the Divine. For the living, you will never have a better calling card.

Celebrate to Beat the Band

Carol Sue, my dear wife of 57 years, was the mother of our two wonderful daughters and the grandmother of our three precious grandchildren. Before she passed away two years ago, we were fortunate to have a Celebration of Life while she was still with us. Unfortunately, Carol Sue's two-year struggle with pancreatic cancer had advanced so far that she was only able to attend the event from afar—Skyped in from a hospital bed as her sister held her hand. Does that sound technical and cold? Not on your life! It's amazing and wonderful that technology exists to build bridges when in-the-flesh experience simply isn't an option.

That said, wouldn't it have been wonderful if Carol Sue's tribute had taken place a little sooner? She responded courageously to the outpouring of love and appreciation, but her senses and awareness were numbed by both medication and advanced disease.

In contrast, how lucky I have been! I have just experienced a series of celebrations with a marked difference. I knew full well that the approaching end was inevitable, but I was gifted with being lucid, completely aware, and able to initiate. Timing and taste are everything. A Celebration of Life is not about prematurely collecting applause after the show is over. **It's all about keeping the dynamics of that which is most precious to us alive for survivors and future generations.**

"These may have been the coldest January days in decades—but the warmth was overpowering."

- Cathy Zacks Gildenhorn

Celebrating the Journey

"For me, it was like being the navigator granted the honor of steering the ship on a blessed journey."

– Cathy

The emcee of a Celebration of Life event sets the tone, and Gordy's daughter, Catherine Zacks Gildenhorn, emceed two of the events. The key is to make it as honest, sincere, and intimate as you can. Identifying the first speaker for each event is a helpful step. That person breaks the ice, and it's easy for others to follow suit. As more and more people attend events of this sort, they become familiar with the spirit and purpose of a Celebration of Life.

"Many of the people who attended one of the three different events we hosted for my dad had earlier been a part of the experience for my mom. When people feel warm and appreciated, it becomes so easy for them to open their hearts. People realize they are there to celebrate life and living, nothing more or nothing less. **For me, it was like being the navigator granted the honor of steering the ship on a blessed journey.**

"When you open your heart and soul to others, you invite them to do the same. After a while, the warmth that's generated can be beautifully inspiring. In my dad's case, these may have been the coldest January days in decades—but the warmth was overpowering."

– Cathy

"*The good people of the world are committed to making it a better place. Gordy has dedicated his life in a focused way. That requires great discipline. Therein may be a lesson for us all.*"

- Jeanie & Jay Schottenstein

Aspire to Wear the Crown of a Good Name

"We learn in the Mishna: 'There are three crowns: the Crown of Torah, the Crown of Priesthood and the Crown of Kingship. But the Crown of a Good Name is superior to them all.' It rises up above the others. Do all the charity and all the good deeds and all the prayer. There's an end-of-life test that Gordy passes so well. Not just that no one has no *bad* things to say about him. It's that others have only *good* things to say about him. At the end of our lives, let us all aspire to wear the Crown of a Good Name in such a way."

- Howard Friedman

One of the great end-of-life lessons is joyful acceptance that life goes on—to have an interest and a dedication to the best possible tomorrow, knowing that one may share in it only in spirit. Be engaged in another person's journey—no matter what age that person may be.

Gordon

For some, Gordon Zacks is—among other amazing things—the man who met the Chabad Lubavitch Rebbe Menachem Schneerson…and not just met him for a minute or two as many did. Their magnetizing hour-and-a-half conversation provided the basis for years of contact.

For those of us who may have the good fortune to enjoy a long and rich life, we could one day be a bridge to a past that can be known through our direct experience. The effect can be sheer magic on the generations we can touch.

A Great Zest for Life

"Our son, Michael, is married to
Gordy's wonderful daughter, Cathy.

"We lovingly call him, 'The Father-in-Law'! Our families
have bonded over the years, sharing children and
grandchildren with great love and joy. Our 'Father-
in-Law's' great zest for life and for worthy causes, his
kindness, enthusiasm, and wisdom have enriched
our lives. What's more, he has been so perceptive in
knowing how people change over time…the Dearfoams®
slippers that Alma receives every holiday season from
him have gone from being sexy…to non-skid!"

- Alma & Joseph Gildenhorn

The Deepest Measure

"Success in life isn't measured by the kind of car you drive or the amount of money you have in the bank…who you know or what you know… The deepest measure known to man is the impact you can have on a young child."

- Howie Goldenfarb

Photo by Leslie Lane Photography

"The deepest measure known to man is the impact you can have on a young child."

- Howie

More than any other force, grandchildren are the spark that has vitalized my later years. Being a grandparent has been the greatest joy in my life.

Being a grandparent has been the greatest joy in my life.

It's really the positive promise and hope of life itself...

Last week my 6-year-old granddaughter Ariela came home and excitedly told me that God had touched her. While she was playing outside, the wind swirled powerfully and took the shape of a man. She felt his arm touch her while he whispered, 'Here are the seeds of a caterpillar that will turn into a butterfly.' She took the seeds, as the wind suddenly vanished. Young children have the most amazing and uncomplicated way of capturing the stages of life. They understand the path from chrysalis to butterfly. We call it metamorphosis, but it's really the positive promise and hope of life itself.

...that keep us alive and make life worth living.

My granddaughter Elissa flew in to give me one more hug...one more kiss. Some might ask: 'Why take an airplane ride for something so small?' Small? What could be more huge? And from my vantage point I can only say, 'What could possibly be more loving and enduring than an act so thoughtful?' End of life alters dramatically how we measure the very things that keep us alive and make life worth living.

Uncle Gordy

"For countless people in our family, Gordy has been *Uncle Gordy* whether he was just a cousin or a blood-line uncle. He has been the person to go to if you want to learn lessons about life and to renew the conviction that the world is indeed your oyster—a realm of endless possibility. In addition to whatever other roles each of us play in life, perhaps we can each aspire to be a trusted, inspirational, educational *Uncle This* or *Aunt That* for the next generation as well."

- Benjy Zacks

"*Perhaps we can each aspire to be a trusted, inspirational, educational* Uncle This *or* Aunt That *for the next generation as well.*"

- Benjy

So many young people have the aptitude,
they just lack the confidence in the
innate, undiscovered ability they already have.

Look for that one moment or special something that can help an individual engage and draw them out. Be that uncle, that special someone who can help young people most of all. Believe in their ability to find their passion and to succeed. So many young people have the aptitude, they just lack the confidence in the innate, undiscovered ability they already have.

I Walk with You Now and Ever as a Brother

"Shortly after the Republican Convention in Detroit in 1980, the nomination firmly settled, my old friend George Bush asked me to meet with one Gordon Zacks to discuss some policy issues. Since I was Reagan's Foreign Policy Advisor, I readily agreed. Of course, I didn't know a Zacks from a Chevrolet.

"Fit and very trim, close-cropped buzzcut, and in a double-breasted blue blazer, Gordon whipped through the door. We moved through the pleasantries; and his first question, asked with a piercing look in his eye, was: 'Can you explain to me why Ronald Reagan has picked a Catholic to deal with the issues of main concern to the Jewish Community in the United States?'

"What an amusing question! After a second, I replied: 'One good reason is that I've done it before in the 1968 Nixon campaign, and the second is that I'm good at it.' That seemed to quiet him for the moment.

"Gordy's been a father confessor, a comrade-in-arms, a true foxhole mate. When I was a target of massive criticism and invasion of my family's privacy, there was Gordy, by the side of me and, more important, of my family.

"Gordy, I walk with you now and ever and as a brother. If there were more Jews who do what you do, just think how much better off we in the Catholic Church would be!

"A Celebration of Life can dramatize some of the most beautiful and disarming incongruities life can offer. Our brotherhood is one of them."

- Dick Allen

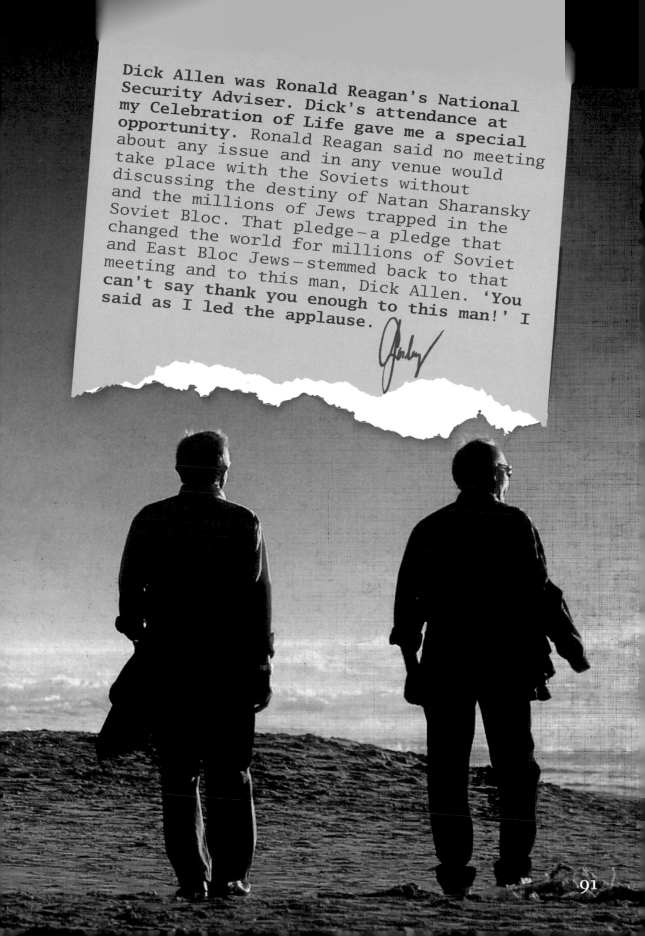

Dick Allen was Ronald Reagan's National Security Adviser. Dick's attendance at my Celebration of Life gave me a special opportunity. Ronald Reagan said no meeting about any issue and in any venue would take place with the Soviets without discussing the destiny of Natan Sharansky and the millions of Jews trapped in the Soviet Bloc. That pledge—a pledge that changed the world for millions of Soviet and East Bloc Jews—stemmed back to that meeting and to this man, Dick Allen. 'You can't say thank you enough to this man!' I said as I led the applause.

A Life Celebration is the opportunity to say a genuine and deeply felt thank you in an unequaled way.

Any person who has the privilege to attend their own Celebration of Life should focus very hard on the people who deserve public gratitude and acknowledgment. No matter who you are and what you have achieved – because what all of us achieve can make a difference far greater than what we can ever imagine – a Life Celebration is the opportunity to say a genuine and deeply felt thank you in an unequaled way.

"I applaud the movement toward Celebrations of Life and a positive recognition instead of accepting a pall over the transition from life to the hereafter — hushed tones, whispered praise, etc. I like this contrasting, bold, open, and celebratory practice."

- Dick Allen

What all of us achieve can
make a difference far greater than
what we can ever imagine.

To Guide, To Teach, To Inspire

"It's no easy task to capture someone who inspires everyone and every type of person so well. Maybe it's the respect he shows others—even in those rare cases when he disagrees with someone or the even rarer cases when he doesn't get along with them. And, he's one hell of a chess player—in all the times we've played, I've only beaten him once. We call him 'Pop Pop.' He can be in the middle of a meeting and his mind a mile away, and you still know he's there for you…that he believes in you unshakably. To guide, to teach, to inspire. That's what this this song is about. I guess that's what life is about, too."

- Edward Gildenhorn

Teacher

(VERSE)
Whenever in doubt
Whatever I'd need
I could always rely on you
To help me

And if
I ever felt alone
I could always find you
On the telephone

And every word you'd say
Would help me win the day

(CHORUS)
Teacher, teacher, teacher,
teach me
About the way life is
And who I can be

Teacher, teacher, teacher,
don't chya know
That you are my hero

(VERSE)
Whether it was
A visit at home
Or the annual trip to Maine

You'd always be
The life of the party
Regardless of your age

And let us not forget
I could barely hold my own
At tennis or chess

(REPEAT CHORUS)

"To guide, to teach, to inspire. That's what this song is about. I guess that's what life is about, too."

- Edward

95

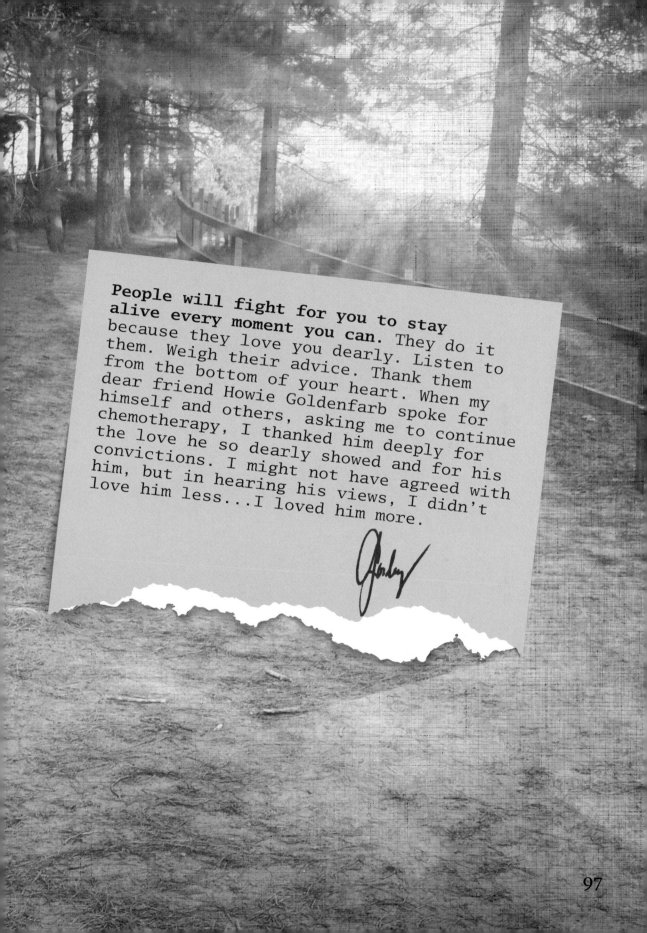

People will fight for you to stay alive every moment you can. They do it because they love you dearly. Listen to them. Weigh their advice. Thank them from the bottom of your heart. When my dear friend Howie Goldenfarb spoke for himself and others, asking me to continue chemotherapy, I thanked him deeply for the love he so dearly showed and for his convictions. I might not have agreed with him, but in hearing his views, I didn't love him less...I loved him more.

97

The Power of Closure

True closure is one of the most powerful treasures in life. It creates stepping stones for us on which we often build the next major advances in our lives. You could be missing closure with someone halfway across the country or someone who's in the next room. **Whatever the barrier may be find the way to break through it.**

A very dear friend of mine was Dr. Judah Folkman. In school, Judah was a year ahead of me. Check that: He was LIGHT YEARS AHEAD OF ME. Judah was perhaps the finest mind ever to come out of Ohio State and may be the finest research talent ever produced by the Harvard Medical School. On January 14, 2008, Judah died in the Denver Airport en route to one of the countless lectures he gave to make cancer research better and wiser. Judah died like my father died. A man of great sensitivities and extraordinary talents – Judah had both – he was ever and systematically achieving closure in all that he did. Yet, I think he might envy me one thing.

The foreknowledge of imminent death has allowed me to plan and to attend to closures. If you have this opportunity, do everything you can not to squander it. As the body deteriorates, each day seems to subtract one physical satisfaction after another. But the satisfaction and rejuvenation one experiences from inching toward closure with the people you love is among the most powerful and rewarding experiences any of us can know.

QUESTIONS TO CONSIDER:
Closure

*1. With whom in your life do you
need to achieve closure?*

*2. Are there lingering tensions or issues
that are obstructing communication?
How can these barriers be overcome?*

*3. If you are in the last stages of life, ask yourself
some questions before you have important
conversations with people you love and care about.*

...ask yourself some questions...

- *Can I boil my main message down to 1-2 key priorities?*

- *Can I make my points relevant to something important going on in the other person's life?*

- *Above all, am I emphasizing the person's strengths and telling them how much they are appreciated?*

4. *How can I open my heart in helping a young person to realize his or her dreams?*

5. *Have I achieved closure with myself about my own contributions and achievements in life? Am I letting myself be sidetracked by guilt, unhappiness, or frustration? Do I instead embrace the constructive things I still might do to make the world a better place?*

*A Tree of Life and Light, a Tree of Wisdom
with an unending passion to teach
and stir the souls of others.*

- Gordy

THE JOY OF THE JOURNEY
FOR OTHERS AND FOR YOURSELF

As his illness advanced, Gordon noticed certain changes in himself. Others noticed them too. His voice became weaker and at times cracked. His thoughts were remarkably clear and lucid, but it required great concentration for him to think through the pain and discomfort. A printed page with a description or course of action might have to be read several times for its meaning to sink in completely. Concentrating on a series of ideas required increasing amounts of energy that had to be alternated with periods of rest, sometimes requiring several hours. You could sense at times that he wished he would have dealt with some administrative details like paying bills or handling certain expenses earlier so he didn't have to dedicate precious energy to them now. To underscore the importance of something— his once powerful grip having become weaker— he would hold on to the hand of the person with whom he was speaking longer and engage in intense eye contact.

Meetings with visitors which were first held with him seated in his executive chair at his desk were then conducted from his wheelchair at the desk. In several days, key meetings would be convened from a wheelchair at the dining room table, but only once or twice a day. Then meetings took place with Gordon on an inflatable-mattress bed in the living room. Despite the marked changes in his vigor—perhaps because he needed boosts to his energy more each day—the hugs of a young granddaughter or the squeeze of a hand seemed to mean more than ever before.

Several days before his death, Gordon called his daughter Catherine to his bedside and said, "Cathy, we've taken the project a remarkable distance together. I've been at the helm as long as I can. I want to continue to look at revisions and additions to the text as it's being assembled. I want to look at proofs of the text ... I want to see the visual layout as it takes shape ... but we both agreed that you would be the best person to ultimately become editor-in-chief. That time has arrived."

The Necessity of Death - A Reflection

My oldest daughter Cathy was 8 years old when my dad died. He was a wonderful grandfather. Cathy loved him dearly. The day after the funeral, Cathy asked me a question: "Dad, why did Grandpa die?"

I answered her: "Sweetheart, I don't know. I'm sure God has a reason and a plan, but he hasn't shared it with me."

The next day, Cathy asked a second question: "Dad, why do good people die?"

Again I replied: "Sweetheart, I don't know. I'm sure God has a plan, but he hasn't shared it with me."

The following day Cathy came to me and said: "...I think I know why people have to die." I looked at my 8-year-old daughter and, this time, I asked her why.

She gave me this remarkable explanation: "Dad, if there was no death, there could be no hope for progress. The world couldn't possibly get better. Everyone and everything would be frozen in yesterday. There'd be nothing new and exciting. Anything better just wouldn't be possible. Death is necessary for the world to get better."

Wow!—from the lips of an 8-year-old...I've never heard a more profound or clearer explanation since. **Death is essential to progress... to change...to the chance to make things better.**

Death is necessary
for the world to get better.

"Can you imagine a more direct, a more noble version of long-range international consequences than that little story of salvation?"

- Tommy

"I'm a first-generation Macedonian American, and I'm the first in my family to make it past the 8th grade. I want to tell you about international relations at the highest level. That's when Gordy cared enough to use his connections with the President of the United States to stir the President to call the Prime Minister of Macedonia. The President makes a phone call so that a two-year-old orphan girl is free to leave for America before she is almost certainly destined for life prostituted into the sex trade. Can you imagine a more direct, a more noble version of long-range international consequences than that little story of salvation? What would the world be like if we all opened our hearts to make world-changing little differences in that very simple, human way?"

– Tommy Taneff

"What would the world be like if we all opened our hearts to make world-changing little differences in that very simple, human way?"

- Tommy

A Pact Made by Friends
to Support a Friend

There are countless ways that we can build bridges to people facing end-of-life situations.

Dov Lautman was one of Israel's great entrepreneurial geniuses and then his life was derailed by ALS. The athlete Lou Gehrig fell to this disease, and most victims expire in 3 to 5 years. The physicist Stephen Hawking has had it for more than half a century. In Dov's case, he struggled with ALS for a decade.

Someone with ALS is usually sentenced to friendless isolation. But, there's a learning beyond that. **A group of Dov's friends got together and they made a pledge. Then they upheld that pledge. Until he died, they swore Dov would neither have lunch nor dinner alone. And, he didn't. For more than a decade...How socially ingenious!** We're not talking about the devotion of family. That itself is vast and wonderful but a bit more fathomable. **This was a pact made by friends to support a friend who had given generously to the world.**

Compared with the remarkable Dov Lautman who suffered with ALS for more than a decade...I have it easy. What are a few uncomfortable, miserable weeks or months compared with ten years of being an aware brain trapped in the prison of a motionless body? It was the *social ingenuity* of his friends who saved Dov from a decade of isolation. There are countless ways that we can build bridges to people facing end-of-life situations, some brief and some very long. **Are we mobilizing our imagination to do what needs to be done to reach and welcome these people and to affirm their humanity?**

You're Never Too Busy to Do the Right Thing by a Friend

On August 2nd 1990, my brother Barry died of cancer at the age of 54. On this day, Iraq invaded Kuwait. At the time, our president was George Herbert Walker Bush.

Do you think that the President of the United States was busy? You *bet* he was! Yet...he found the time to call me and to express his condolences. He also called my brother's widow on her loss.

What kind of man does this? Probably the kindest, most decent, most compassionate man I ever met.

An unforgettable lesson for living: The President of the United States...on the day that our ally Kuwait is invaded...found the time **to do the right thing by a friend.**

Take time to be personal when a friend or a loved one is in need. That's an art George H.W. Bush practices with unrivaled skill. He effortlessly telescopes his sincere attention from the world stage to the kitchen table, as intimate as he is expansive.

Make this pledge to yourself: **Never be too busy to do the right thing by a friend**. The finality, the irreversibility of death drives home that imperative

an unforgettable lesson for living

more than any other force I know. How *you* will be remembered is often driven by how you remember others. Don't do it to simply satisfy expectations. Do it because **remembering others sustains and elevates the dignity of us all.**

A couple of days ago, in January 2014, George Herbert Walker Bush called again. He might not have been steering the ship of state in the White House, but he certainly still had enough to think about. His wife Barbara had just returned from a hospitalization. This time he dialed up my number to talk about me. He knew I was in a tough corner, but he's not one to give up on a fight. Nor am I. So **his call helped to make me even more determined to put the time I had to good use.**

It's all about the struggle. Inherent to Judaism is an acceptance that we will never be able to resolve all the challenges that lie before us. But, with the confidence and support of those who love us, we can make the all-important little dents that make the world a better place.

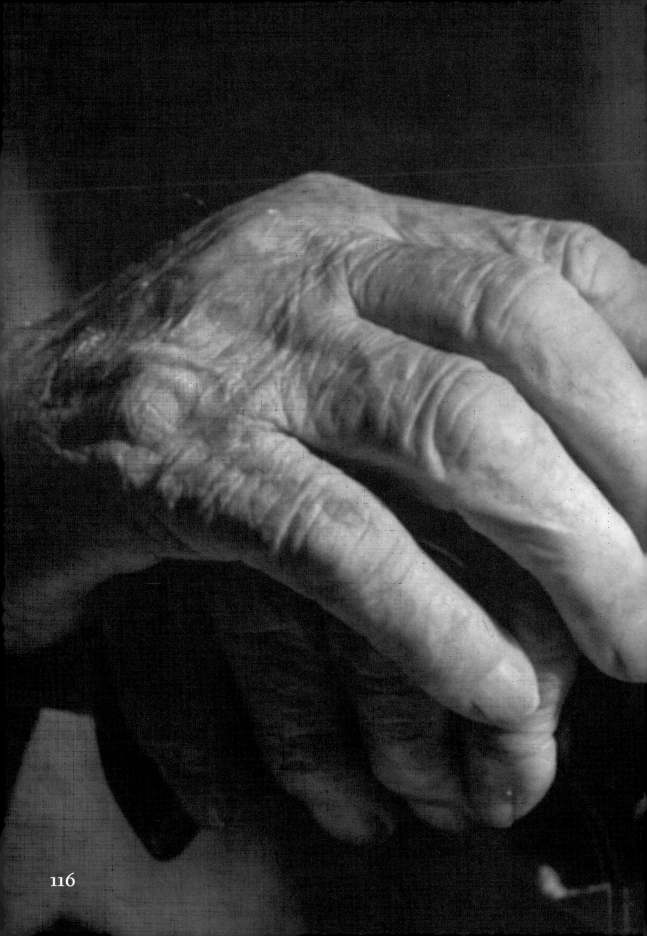

Dignity Comes from God, Not Man

Dignity comes from God, not man. My friend Natan Sharansky once said to me: "No other human being can take another person's dignity away. Only you can give your dignity to another." What strength that conviction gave Natan, freezing in that gulag icebox and refusing to relent to inexhaustible attempts by the Soviets to strip him of his dignity. Through connecting his own predicament with the legacy of Jewish history, he not only survived, but he pioneered a new mindset that brought us to a richer level of personal purpose and meaning.

When did I first accept an end-of-life situation could be so humbling? I didn't learn it because of what's happening to me right now. This took place more than a couple of years ago when my wife Carol was gravely ill with pancreatic cancer—a cancer like mine that proved fatal. As her illness deepened, we saw the best doctors in the world. No stone was left unturned. Yet there was nothing that could be done. I felt so helpless. Before that moment, any challenge in life had always seemed to hinge on finding a *better* answer. Suddenly there was no better answer. There was no way her condition was going to improve medically. And one needs to recognize the clock is ticking.

Suddenly there was no better answer. There was no way her condition was going to improve medically. And one needs to recognize the clock is ticking.

Humiliation and Acceptance

One of the most challenging aspects of the end of life is the devastating loss of independence in doing the very simplest things—moving yourself, dressing yourself, caring for yourself. It may require tapping powerful new reservoirs of humility and acceptance to realign your attitudes and to keep yourself motivated. Because, as new and as challenging as these outlooks may be, they are equally indispensable **across the board** to getting things done...and to enjoying the moment. Both are very real possibilities at the end of life, so you have to be prepared to do things in new ways.

Man doesn't give dignity to man. God does. If it's God who confers dignity on man, it's up to each of us to overcome the humiliation when we suffer a perceived affront. Every one of us dreads the loss of dignity as we enter life's final stages. Perhaps we fear this assault (and insult) on *whom we think we are* like no other abuse. What do you expect my answer to you would have been a year ago, if you had asked me:

- *Would you use a walker?*

- *Would you be willing to be carted around in a wheelchair?*

- *And—maybe the ultimate—would you be willing to wear an adult disposable diaper?*

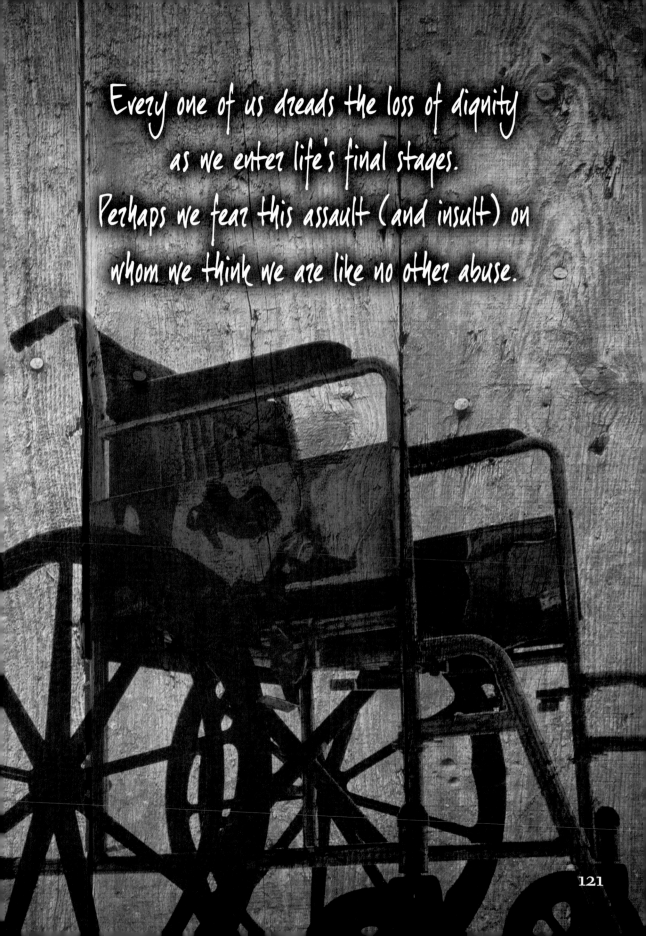

Every one of us dreads the loss of dignity
as we enter life's final stages.
Perhaps we fear this assault (and insult) on
whom we think we are like no other abuse.

Our struggle to preserve our independence
and our perceived identity is often
waged on the battleground of dignity.

I would have laughed at each of these options... and probably with considerable scorn. Now I pragmatically accept each measure because these are all tools I need to serve a bigger objective.

The seminal issue: **_Our struggle to preserve our independence and our perceived identity is often waged on the battleground of dignity._** Civility and dignity are not a game of appearance. They're not about which fork you use. It's about how you exploit whatever resources you have to make a positive difference. If tools can help, embrace them, don't resist them.

Don't even view these measures as concessions. Don't start negotiating with Death. You can't let Death define your endgame. But you **_must_** be prepared to **_redefine_** yourself—who you have become and what you are capable of today—if you want to stay in charge of your own agenda, no matter what it may be: seeing your garden grow, hugging your grandkids, or dotting the i's on a farewell note to your board of directors.

The end of life doesn't strip us of dignity. The last stages of life do assault our hubris. And smile: If an astronaut is prepared to wear a Maximum Absorbency Garment (an intergalactic _Depends_) on a long-distance spacewalk to do his or her job, why shouldn't you do the same to achieve what you need to do? Your willingness to accept perceived "humiliation" will often be directly related to your opportunities to experience joy. _Live life as it's available to you and relish it!_

As a part-time job during our student days, my brother and I used to do gigs as magicians. Once I was asked to do a magic act as part of the birthday celebration for my 5-year-old nephew. Some of my routines were getting stale, so I decided to try out a totally new number. I asked for a volunteer, and of course the volunteer was the little nephew, sporting a brand-new, perfectly pressed blue serge suit. The trick: The magician pours a pitcher of milk down a magic funnel that is created out of today's newspaper. The nephew had a troubled look on his face. "Uncle Gordy...I think there's a problem," he said. The milk was supposed to disappear from the funnel into thin air, actually channeled through a tube attached to the pitcher itself. Instead, it was gushing down his leg and ruining the birthday boy's suit!

The experience taught me two indelible lessons: **Preparation for anything is everything. And always have a Plan B up your sleeve to deal with the unexpected.** In the final stages of life, you encounter unexpected changes every day. Constantly prepare yourself to regroup, and you will always have the upper hand.

Ruining the
Birthday Boy's Suit

*In the final stages of life, you encounter
unexpected changes every day.*

QUESTIONS TO CONSIDER:
Personal Energy Goals

1. Have I rewritten my 'bucket list' of what I want to achieve given both the time available and my physical ability to actually do what I would like to do?

2. Do I regularly reassess what I am trying to do for the best impact and most enjoyable and rewarding results?...Or am I wasting valuable time in a struggle to do things that are no longer possible or must be done in a different way?

3. Am I realistic and accepting that my strength and physical options are likely to deteriorate… and that I must re-calibrate? For example, are things that were perfectly possible a week or a month ago possible today?

4. Am I asking loved ones to be my mirrors? Are friends and family asked to signal you when you need to rest? Are they there to help you with those nuisances that were once a snap and that are now both traps and trials?

5. How can I be "socially ingenious" in helping to energize others in innovative ways?

"Every moment counts!
Every word counts!
Everything counts!"

- Michael Gildenhorn

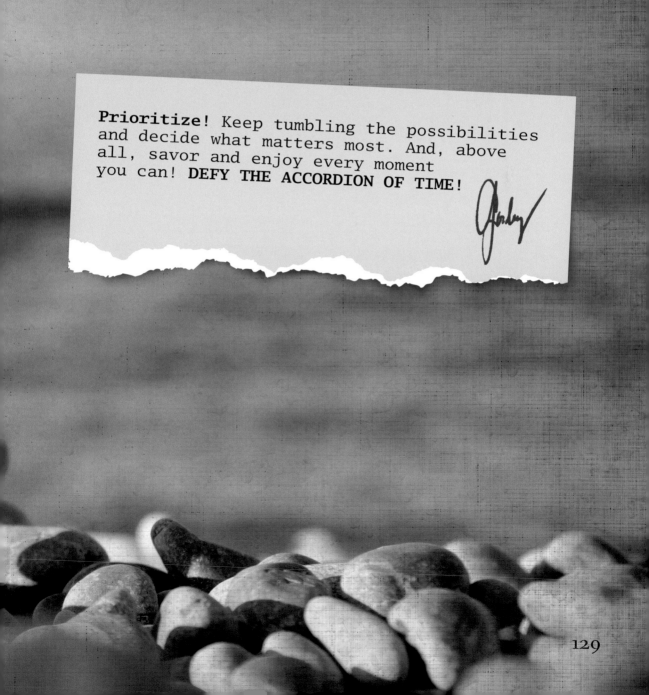

Prioritize! Keep tumbling the possibilities and decide what matters most. And, above all, savor and enjoy every moment you can! **DEFY THE ACCORDION OF TIME!**

Personal Energy
Booster Tips

1. *Do I try to match the day's activities to my body's biological clock? For example, if I'm most alert and vigorous in the mornings, do I reserve the day's most important activities for these high-energy times?*

2. *Do I have an opportunity to be around young people and children? Not only can the experience be irreplaceably cherished by the young people, it has a wonderfully stimulating and uplifting energy that can be a powerful energizer for your psyche. Young children are perhaps the purest embodiment of love and spontaneity that any of us can know.*

3. Am I trying to give birth to a full-gown man overnight? If you've postponed writing War and Peace *or painting the ceiling of the Sistine Chapel until the day you get some very bad news, don't start now. By the way, the comedian Jackie Mason once quipped that he and his brother-in-law could have done that ceiling in a day and a half, if they only had a couple of rollers. Define what's doable and do it well!*

4. Am I tanking up and recharging? You can't get very far without energy. Are you nibbling at the things you like, even if you eat sparingly? Are you vigilant about keeping yourself hydrated?

EPILOGUE

THE TREE OF LIFE

Help the Tree of Life Blossom

In Judaism, the concept of *Tzedakah* is the obligation to perform acts of kindness and good deeds. Rabbi Abraham Joshua Heschel, who passed in 1972, was one of the foremost Jewish philosopher-theologians of the 20th century. I was blessed to spend Saturday afternoon upon afternoon at his Riverside Avenue apartment in Manhattan. Sitting on the floor among students and colleagues, we were all gifted by his wondrous outpourings.

The unending stream of wisdom and energy in his ideas was as though The Tree of Life and Light had taken root right before us. Heschel saw life as a pattern and he insisted that ideas of goodness be authentically rendered in acts of goodness. Heschel didn't just applaud Martin Luther King in his quest for racial equality. Heschel marched with King. Heschel not only taught about the essence of time, his very lessons were a model of time itself.

*The Tree of Life and Light had
taken root right before us.*

- Gordy

*Life has no higher purpose than to nourish
the Tree and grow fruit for the world.*

- Gordy

Heschel taught that Judaism was a religion of time, not space. Time was for him amoeba-like. Invest it well in teaching and sharing with others, and the goodness of the investment would multiply itself. The goodness would be self-replicating. How much like a Tree of Life was Heschel's universe—this blending together of light and growth. How compelling, rejuvenating, and life-affirming Heschel's image of the world—this dazzling light-channeling Tree of Wisdom with an unending passion to teach and stir the souls of others. What an enticing and sturdy affirmation of life I find this image to be as my journey reaches its goal. **The universal message of the Jewish story is to think beyond yourself: Don't just pluck fruit of The Tree of Life yourself.** Life has no higher purpose than to nourish The Tree and grow fruit for the world.

Carrying the Torch

AN AFTERWORD
Catherine Zacks Gildenhorn

My dad finished writing this book in less than a month. It was only then that he allowed himself to rest. Our family and Gale were with him early in the morning on February 1, 2014 when he passed.

After he received the medical diagnosis of terminal cancer, Dad was in great pain, and he didn't have much time. As he struggled to make sense of this looming deadline, he realized that encountering the end of life was a time of great insight—and that people of all ages could benefit from that perspective.

After a lifetime of purposeful living, my father also realized that writing this book would be one of his final projects. Indeed he already had additional projects in mind if he were permitted the time and wherewithal to pursue them. From the first stages of the book's conception, he had asked me to be prepared to step in and take on the responsibility for finishing the project. Because he would not be able to complete the details of publication and represent the book before the media, he asked me to serve as its spokesperson. He wanted this book to be a useful resource for the public—and he therefore understood that the book needed a living ambassador. I agreed to play that role.

My dad was associated with R. G. Barry Corporation for more than sixty years, much of that time as its Chief Executive Officer. While he was proud to lead and grow the company my grandparents had started, he pursued a purpose in life far beyond business. His overall vision was to make the world a better place.

For years, my father was intensely active and passionately involved in:

- The State of Israel and the American-Israel Relationship,
- The American Jewish Community,
- Leadership Development Programs, and
- Continuing Jewish Education.

His commitment to Continuing Education advanced a tradition begun by his deeply loved mother—my wonderful grandmother—Florence Zacks Melton.

My dad pursued these passions for decades. He also had the awareness to help defining moments happen when they suddenly presented themselves. He advised American presidents and Israeli prime ministers. He helped liberate Russian dissidents like Natan Sharansky, an event that helped topple the Soviet Union. And he played a key role in developing the American Jewish Community's top young leadership programs.

My dad guest lectured extensively on Leadership at various prestigious universities including Harvard's Kennedy School of Government, the Harvard School of Business, and the Fox School of Business at Temple University.

It was a great honor to be entrusted with editing this book. I also had the privilege to emcee several of his Celebration of Life events. These took place at our Columbus home in January 2014 during the coldest days we had known in decades. But these gatherings with friends and family were filled with love and transformed into the warmest days imaginable.

My involvement in my father's mission of advocacy for end-of-life issues was ultimately a blessing: It prevented me from being paralyzed by sadness and grief. We were just so busy living. That is exactly how Dad wanted it.

From its inception, *Redefining Moments* has been intended as seed material for a website. This Internet derivation of the book is open to everyone at *www.RedefiningMoments.org*. Visitors to the site will have the opportunity to resource ideas and contribute their own experiences. The overall objective is to create an organic "end-of-life" reservoir of knowledge and information. Sponsored by the Jewish National Fund, the website *www.RedefiningMoments.org* is available to people of all faiths and backgrounds.

My dad believed that sharing end-of-life issues was a vital opportunity to realizing the full potential for both love and purposeful living. He was very much attracted to the opportunities of information sharing built up from the grassroots level. The website operates in that spirit. It does not offer medical information, but rather helps people learn about attitudes, motivations and goals in life. **It is intended as a sort of DIGITAL ETERNAL FLAME carrying on my father's spirit and values.**

L'Chaim, dear Dad, with all my love, admiration and respect. **We will do our best to nurture your legacy so that it blossoms and grows.**

"L'Chaim, dear Dad, with all my love, admiration and respect."

- Cathy

140

About the Editor

Catherine Zacks Gildenhorn

Catherine Zacks Gildenhorn, Gordon Zacks' eldest daughter, has been intimately involved in the development of this book, and serves as its Editor-in-Chief. Additionally, she emceed the Celebration of Life events dedicated to her father and was specifically asked by him to be the book's spokesperson and advocate going forward.

Born in Columbus, Ohio, Catherine Zacks Gildenhorn has lived in the Washington DC area for over twenty years. No stranger to public life, she serves on the Board and Executive Committee of the Jewish Federation of Greater Washington and on the National Women's Philanthropy Board. She also served as a Presidential Appointee to the United States Holocaust Memorial Council.

Catherine Zacks Gildenhorn is a graduate of the University of Michigan and Emory University School of Law. She lives in Bethesda with her husband Michael, her children Edward and Elissa, and her two golden retrievers Toby and Tyler.

FREQUENTLY ASKED QUESTIONS

What's the objective of *Redefining Moments*?

"End of life: Death will be no stranger for any of us. Coming to terms with end of life early and constructively can release considerable positive energy. It also helps many people grapple with significant life planning." - Gordy

Two of the book's foremost objectives are to help people better achieve the joy and closure that end-of-life experiences can provide and to encourage both urgency and thoughtfulness in grappling with life-planning priorities.

When did Gordon Zacks decide to write this book?

His decision to dedicate his remaining days to the writing of *Redefining Moments* came after he received a diagnosis of terminal prostate liver cancer in December 2013. An evaluation by his doctor provided the news that he had just weeks to live. Gordon already knew he had prostate cancer for several years, and it seemed to be pursuing an unhurried course. Unfortunately, the cancer had changed its behavior and migrated to his liver.

It should be noted that life planning issues had already been an area of intense interest for him and that he treated the topic in his earlier book *Defining Moments,* published in 2006.

Why does closure occupy such a central role in end-of-life considerations?

If you're facing an end-of-life situation with a loved one, get to that bedside. Chances are your need for closure may be greater than you might recognize. Chances are you'll remember this for the rest of your life and it may change your life. Chances are you'll never have another chance.

Does the author recommend people should do bold and dramatic things when they realize the end of life is upon them?

"Stay true to your purpose in life and its value." - Gordy

If the opportunity exists, rewrite your "bucket list" to achieve realistic goals given both the time available and the physical ability to do what you would like to do.

Don't try to give birth to a full-grown man overnight. Define what's doable and do it well.

Who will benefit financially from the publication of this book?

As with Gordon Zacks' first book, any author profits will be directed to charity, in this case to the American Hebrew Academy and the Jewish National Fund.

Does this little book contain all the answers one needs to know to be prepared to face the end of life?

No. Gordon Zacks expressly intended this book as a starting point and a launching pad for initiating dialogue about end-of-life issues and concerns. His book is a major initial entrant in a new, interactive website established and maintained by the Jewish National Fund for people of all affiliations and outlooks. The website *www.RedefiningMoments.org* both shares information and allow individuals to post experiences and comments which may benefit others.

Why might humility be so important to successful living in end-of-life situations?

"One of the most challenging aspects of the end of life is the devastating loss of independence in doing the very simplest things—moving yourself, dressing yourself, caring for yourself. It may require tapping powerful new reservoirs of humility and acceptance to realign your attitudes and to keep yourself motivated ... Your willingness to accept perceived 'humiliation' will often be directly related to your opportunities to experience joy. Live life as it's available to you and relish it!" - Gordy

Has Gordon Zacks designated any representative to act as a spokesperson for themes in the book going forward?

His daughter, Catherine Zacks Gildenhorn, was actively involved in the editing of this book and in coordinating and emceeing the Celebration of Life events for her father. Gordy Zacks requested and Cathy accepted the role of champion and advocate for principles articulated in *Redefining Moments*.

Gordon B. Zacks:
A PERSONAL CHRONOLOGY

March 11, 1933	Gordon Zacks is born.
1946	Gordon and his family move to Columbus, Ohio.
May 14, 1948	The independent State of Israel is declared.
1948	The firm R. G. Barry is established.
1951	After failing to gain admission to Harvard, Gordon enters Dartmouth.
December 19, 1954	Gordon and Carol Sue marry.
1955	Gordon graduates from Ohio State University.
1955	Gordon joins R. G. Barry.
1961	The United Jewish Appeal Young Leadership Cabinet is established with Gordon as Founder and Chairman.
1965	Gordon becomes President of R. G. Barry.
September 29, 1965	Aaron Zacks, Gordon's father, passes.
June 5, 1967	The "Six-Day War" begins.
1969	Gordon delivers a keynote address to the Council of Jewish Federations and Welfare Funds Annual Conference.
October 5-26, 1973	The "Yom Kippur War" takes place.
1976	Gordon becomes National Vice Chairman of the Jewish Coalition for Ford/Dole Presidential Campaign.
1978	Natan Sharanksy is imprisoned in the Soviet Union.
1979	Gordon becomes Chairman of the Board of R. G. Barry.
May 28, 1981	Gordon helps to arrange and attends a pivotal meeting with President Reagan and Avital Sharansky at the White House.
February 11, 1986	Natan Sharansky is released from Soviet prison.
December 6, 1987	Vice President George Bush delivers the "Let My People Go" speech at the Freedom Sunday Rally for Soviet Jewry on the Washington Mall.

1987-1988	Gordon co-chairs the Bush for President Finance Committee.
1988	Gordon is Chairman of the Bush for President National Jewish Campaign Committee.
1988	George H. W. Bush is elected 41st U.S. President.
August 3, 1990	Barry Zacks, Gordon's brother, passes.
1992	Gordon is Vice-Chairman of the Bush/Quayle National Finance Committee.
1993	Gordon is named to the Board of Trustees of the George Bush Presidential Library.
June 2002	Gordon becomes Chairman of the Florence Melton Adult Mini-School.
2004	Gordon retires from R. G. Barry.
2006	Gordon's book *Defining Moments* is published.
2006-2013	Gordon conducts leadership seminars at several prestigious American universities.
February 8, 2007	Florence Zacks Melton, Gordon's mother, passes.
2008	Gordon launches the Defining Moments Society for leadership development and remains active in this initiative through the end of his life.
2009-2012	Gordon's wife, Carol Sue, develops terminal pancreatic cancer in 2009 and passes in 2012.
January 2011	Gordon learns he has prostate cancer.
October 25, 2011	Gordon delivers TEDx Talk at Claremont College.
December 18, 2013	Gordon is diagnosed with terminal prostate liver cancer.
January 7 & 9, 2014	Gordon hosts Celebration of Life events at his home.
January 13, 2014	Gordon begins writing *Redefining Moments*.
February 1, 2014	Gordon's passes.
February 3, 2014	Memorial Service for Gordon takes place in Columbus, Ohio.
May 2014	*www.RedefiningMoments.org* launches.

GORDON BENJAMIN ZACKS

בנימין בן אהרן ובלומא

d. February 1, 2014 / 1 Adar I, 5774
Memorial Service Remarks by Rabbi Harold J. Berman

In his last days, as many people came to say good-bye, Gordon Zacks kept saying: "I'm the luckiest guy that was ever born." He felt lucky and truly blessed, for things he could not control, for being born to two remarkable parents, for being a Jew in a generation when important things were happening to the Jewish people, for being an American at a critical moment in American history, and for having had opportunities to make a real difference as history unfolded around him.

He felt lucky because, as much as anything else, he loved giving, helping, using his resources and his talents to make thing better for others and to inspire others to do more for those around them. As long as Gordon Zacks could do those things, there was purpose in his life, so he never stopped doing those things until he had literally exhausted every ounce of strength in his body.

He left us on Shabbat, Shabbat Terumah, the Shabbat on which we read in the Torah about giving. The word Terumah, the name of the Torah reading, means in Biblical Hebrew and in modern Hebrew "gift." And we gather to express our gratitude for so many gifts that are ours because of Gordon Zacks.

To his family, Gordy was the man everyone turned to, for anything. He always seemed to be there when needed. For his daughters, for his grandchildren, for nieces and nephews (and nieces and nephews included cousins and lots of others), he was the totally dedicated family man who didn't solve problems for people as much as he helped people, and showed people, how to solve problems on their own. He didn't want to just fix something. He wanted to give people the self-confidence to turn their own lives around. He, himself, was totally comfortable being who he was. He was, as we all know, very sure of himself. His own term: he was an "in your face" kind of guy. He didn't necessarily want everyone else to be, but he wanted that sense of purpose and that kind of personal direction for everyone around him.

As a community leader, Gordy was a force to be reckoned with in every setting. He never left people in doubt as to where he stood and he hardly ever took "no" for an answer. Eloquent and charismatic, Gordy could, and regularly did, hold audiences spell bound. No one who listened to a Gordon Zacks speech or participated in a Gordon Zacks seminar ever forgot it.

As a business leader, Gordy was creative and energetic, taking the company his parents had started and building it into a major international enterprise. Yet he never stopped caring about each and all the people who worked for R. G. Barry, all those, not only in Columbus but around the world as well, who looked to him for their well-being and their livelihood. He never took any responsibility lightly.

Yet, through it all, Gordy could laugh at himself, could be silly, could play with his girls and even more with his grandchildren. He loved music. He loved to dance. He loved to have fun. He loved life.

As said, Gordy was grateful, all through life, for lessons learned from his parents. His mother, Florence Zacks Melton, was interested in everything, taught him and all of us how to think out of the box, and pushed him to learn from every experience. He adored and respected her and never stopped trying to make her proud. His dad, Aaron Zacks, who passed away much too young, had been his mentor and role model. As a self assured youngster, Gordy thought he could do anything and everything. His dad gave him the chance to prove himself, and when Gordy stumbled, his dad showed him how to learn from mistakes and grow into true leadership.

Gordy loved his family. His brother Barry was so different, in appearance, style, politics, but they treasured and looked out for each other, and, after Barry died, Gordy felt a huge responsibility for rest of the family.

Of course, most of all, he adored Carol Sue. As a college student, it was love at first sight. He had finished two years at Dartmouth, but he wasn't going to risk going that far away when he was in love. He transferred to OSU, and they were married before he graduated. She was all of eighteen. They grew together, faced challenges of all kinds, traveled all over the world, respected each other's skills and talents and depended on each other for all the things that really mattered. When Carol Sue was sick, Gordy put his whole life on hold, moved to Boston and devoted himself to seeing that she had the best care in the world. Nothing was more important.

Gordy reached adulthood in the aftermath of World War II. He grew up seeing the price that had been paid for Jewish vulnerability and for what he saw as American Jewish passivity. A teenager when Israel became a nation, Gordy resolved to do everything in his power to help Jews, everywhere, to fight anti-Semitism and to strengthen the State of Israel.

He got involved as a young leader in the Columbus Jewish Community, then became one of the founders and organizers of the National Young Leadership Cabinet of what was then the United Jewish Appeal. At a very young age, his passion and power in public speaking were remarkable. National organizations sought him out for leadership positions. Then Gordy got involved in politics, not for personal ego, but for results. He met powerful world leaders, prime ministers and presidents, and it was all important to him, not for prestige, but for possibility. He wanted to help Jews trying to leave the former Soviet Union and he was proud to have placed that on Ronald Reagan's agenda and to have followed through with Presidents Reagan and Bush. He wanted to make sure America always stood by Israel. He wanted America and Israel to stand together for morality, for human progress and for peace. He met, many times, prime ministers and presidents, but he was not intimidated, by anyone, and he was not prepared to give up on any cause he thought worthwhile.

His daughters, Cathy and Kim, and his whole extended family, looked up to him, in every way. The memories of big things, and of little things, the stories he told, the connections he made, gave focus to their lives and their life commitments and he was there for them. When needed, he would drop everything and run, literally, to be at their side. Cathy married Michael, and brought Edward and Elissa into his life. Kim's daughter, Ariela, gave him another new focus of love. For all the big things Gordy did, he always let them know that their love was the most important thing in his life.

At age 70 he stepped down from actively running R. G. Barry, although he continued to serve as Chairman. That gave him more time to speak and to write, to chair the Florence Melton Mini-School program his mother had started and to develop the Defining Moments Society. He took people who had talent and were already leaders and challenged them to look at their lives, goals and ultimate legacies. He gathered people from all over North America, brought them to Israel, introduced them to each other and left an indelible imprint on all their lives.

And when, at age 80, just over the past few months, he realized that days were numbered, Gordy only wanted to do more. He wrote another book, and where he got the strength we will never know. He gathered people in his home and let them know how much he appreciated them, and many of them, having come together from all over the world, shared stories of what Gordy had done for them and how he had inspired them.

At the end, it was Cathy and Kim with their dad, the dad who had always seemed larger than life, who taught them to do and be their best, whose hugs made them feel safe and loved. Ariela was there. Michael and Edward and Elissa were always close. Gordy pushed himself to the very end because pushing himself was the only way he knew. He never did, and never would, just sit and wait for things to happen. Now Gordy has met his Maker; we only hope his Maker is prepared.

As said, he left us on Shabbat. Parshat Terumah. The Torah portion talks about taking what you have and sharing generously so the community around you will be something better. Now there is much left before us and we will always remember how he urged us to action, pushed us toward defining moments and challenged us to make the world a better place.

We offer our sympathy to Cathy and Michael and Kim, to Edward, Elissa and Ariela, to the whole Zacks family, to Gordy's assistant, Amanda, and to all whose lives were touched by a truly remarkable man.

תהי נשמתו צרורה בצרור החיים

May his soul be bound up in the bond of life.

זכרונו לברכה

May his memory always be a blessing.

Texts of additional tributes and eulogies spoken at the Memorial Service and at the graveside for Gordon Zacks in Columbus, Ohio on February 3, 2014 can be found at the website *www.RedefiningMoments.org*

These profoundly moving remarks were made by:

- The Honorable John Richard Kasich, Governor of Ohio,

- The Honorable Richard V. Allen, former National Security Adviser to President Ronald Reagan and fellow of Hoover Institution,

- His Excellency Natan Sharansky, Israeli human rights activist and author.

" תהי נשמתו צרורה בצרור החיים

*May his soul be bound up
in the bond of life.*

זכרונו לברכה

*May his memory always
be a blessing.* "

- Rabbi Harold J. Berman

ACKNOWLEDGMENTS

*Made on Gordon Zacks' behalf
by his daughter Catherine Zacks Gildenhorn*

Senator Joseph Lieberman's willingness to write such a beautifully articulated introduction on such short notice was gracious beyond words. Our thanks go out to Beaufort publisher Eric Kampmann and managing editor Megan Trank for taking on this ambitious project on such short notice and for dedicating themselves to both a quality result and a quick turnaround timetable, remarkable within the publishing industry. Arthur Klebanoff represented my dad in his first book, *Defining Moments*. As a courtesy, he graciously helped us with remarkably authoritative insights into the world of publishing in the preparation of *Redefining Moments*. Michelle Rousseau Laytner and her graphic team, including Rebecca Luttrell, Caroline Bounds, and Allysa Wolf, did an exceptionally fine job of capturing the graphic dimension of the book, including many hours of selecting supporting photography and directing the overall graphic program that has given *Redefining Moments* its distinctive look. And, finally I am eternally grateful to our insightful collaborator Ron Beyma for his boundless dedication. Without him, this project would not have been possible.

As always, Gordon's Executive Assistant Amanda Piergiovanni has done the extraordinary in supporting my dad, and, in particular, in aiding in the completion of this book. Her unflagging attention to detail came at a particularly trying time, as she was primary caregiver to a terminal cancer victim, a loved one in her own family. This makes her dedication and diligence all the more remarkable.

Jesse Sage provided invaluable insight and perspective in his reading of interim drafts. I also wish to thank Russell Robinson and the Jewish National Fund for their constant support and for their special role in working with Ezra Chasser and his team in the construction and management of the *Redefining Moments* website, *www.RedefiningMoments.org*

Gale Shamansky, my dad's companion, not only provided keen observations that improved the book, but also helped us make sure my dad's wish of completing the book was realized, despite the considerable demands this made on their private time of his closing days. My sister Kim's role in this enterprise was immeasurable. While lovingly and intensively aiding with our dad's care in his final weeks, she made time to help search through her extensive library of family photos in a quest for the right images, helped organize videos of the Celebration of Life events so they could be easily accessed for citation, assisted in editing the manuscript, and offered perceptive suggestions on how the overall book concept could benefit by adding important elements—especially regarding my dad's dedication to family. I am also indebted to Dr. Steven Clinton for his invaluable help in explaining the nature of my dad's illness found both on the book jacket and in the Frequently Asked Questions.

All those who were cited in the book were incredibly understanding and prompt, working with our accelerated publication timetable. Randy Zacks did a fine job of capturing the video images of the Celebration of Life events, extensively cited in the text. Household stalwarts Victoria Murphy and drivers James and Kathryn Payne were ever ready to help with logistic support for the book as they were dedicated to the continuing demands imposed by the steady stream of visitors to our dad's home during his final weeks.

I also want to add a deep thank you to my loving husband Michael and my two wonderful children, Elissa and Edward. My constant supporters, they enabled me, in this case, to relocate to Columbus to spend these cherished moments with my dad and to take on the duties of editing this book and advocating its messages—a cause about which my dad felt so passionately.

INDEX

PHOTO/ART CREDITS

157